A LETTER
TO MY FRESHMAN SELF
THIRD EDITION

A LETTER
TO MY FRESHMAN SELF
THIRD EDITION

A LETTER TO MY FRESHMAN SELF
Third Edition

Copyright © 2021 by Glynn Family Honors Program Notre Dame

10 9 8 7 6 5 4 3 2 1

ISBN 978-1-7352702-5-8

Published by
Corby Books
A Division of Corby Publishing LP
P.O. Box 93
Notre Dame, Indiana 46556

Manufactured in the United States of America

PREFACE

In the summer of 2019, on a grueling road trip from Los Angeles to New York City, my mother requested that we exit the Indiana toll road towards Notre Dame. After hours of driving past monotonous flat plains, a brief walk around St. Mary's Lake and the Grotto was a welcome respite. Months later, amid a worsening pandemic, I would reminisce of how normal and how calming this visit had been, and in seeking this solace, I committed to Notre Dame. In the past year, Notre Dame staked out a less-taken path to bring most of its student body back onto campus for in-person class attendance. Those two semesters were filled with more than just the usual pressures from academics, relationships, and unfamiliarity. Students also grappled with the coronavirus, an uncertain economic future, public health measures, societal reckoning, mental health, and an increased sense of isolation. I hope that this anthology—combining letters from a time before and during the Covid-19 pandemic—will encourage current and future generations of Domers, through past experiences and solidarity, to firmly confront their struggles and take advantage of their time here under the dome.

To Felicity Wong, Ciara Fay, Garrett Pacholl, Santosh Ponna, Aidan Meuninck, Brooke Rodriguez, and Saachi Kumar, I am deeply grateful for our collaboration. Thank you for the time spent finding, discussing, and refining the content that ultimately crafted this book. I would also like to thank Alex 'Xiaotong' Lin, the talented artist and friend who painted the inspiring cover artwork. The tulips are symbolic of spring and rejuvenation after a harsh winter.

To Professor Bahram Moasser, thank you for our spontaneous conversations and invaluable guidance that first fostered the creation of this 3rd edition. To Professor Christopher Kolda, thank you for the vital guidance, advice, and support that you have bestowed on our editorial team throughout the journey of creating this book. We would also like to thank the Glynn Family Honors Program and the Glynn Family for their backing of this book. To Jim Langford and Michael Brown, our publishers at Corby Books, thank you for accompanying and guiding us on this book-creating process.

To Haley Kempf, Lily Kang, and the editorial teams of the first and second editions, we are incredibly grateful to you for setting a precedent and allowing us to inherit this project and evolve it for future Domers. We hope to pass on the torch to future classes to craft their edition of this book.

Finally, I am greatly appreciative to the Notre Dame students, current and alumnus, who contributed or considered contributing to this third edition. Your humility and wisdom will push future students to thrive in times of difficulty and make our world a better place.

In Notre Dame,

Jin Rui Cai
CLASS OF 2024

TABLE OF CONTENTS

What If

Dear freshman Emily,

It's easy to get lost in the what-ifs. There are far too many of them, and when you struggle with anxiety that can bring you to your knees, there's infinitely more. When we look back at the year behind us, a year of sorrow, of fear, of desperate cries for justice, of defeat, of loneliness, of darkness, the what-ifs come pouring in like a waterfall of regret and anger, saturating your body and mind with a cold weight.

What if we could have stopped this? What if she hadn't died? What if I could have done something better? What if I didn't help them enough? What if things will never be the same? What if something happens to him? What if I can't handle this? What if this proves I am weak, not strong?

In the midst of rebuilding myself from the wreckage of an abusive relationship, with my anxiety biting at my ankles as I trudged along, the pandemic hit the fragile walls I had painstakingly pieced back together like a truck careening down an ice-covered hill.

What's worst about the what-ifs is that they not only torment you from within—they also make it impossible to expel them.

What if she thinks I'm crazy? What if they think I'm a disappointment? What if this makes me an awful person?

but in times as difficult as those we've battled in the past year, there were people brave enough to share their words, their struggles, their stories, even when their voices shook. I looked at these people, at the troubled world, and I wondered about what might happen if I met each one of my scary what-ifs with a question full of hope and joy as these people had found the courage to do so.

and if so,

what if

I smile at everyone I pass in the street. I share my story in hopes it will help someone else. I hug all of my friends as much as I can. I overuse the phrase "I love you." I read too many books. I keep precious memories alive through my writing. I wake up each morning and whisper "I am thankful to be alive."

When I do those things, I feel the what-ifs that lie heavy on my shoulders begin to melt, and I feel something other than numbness.

After years of battling my what-ifs, and after a year of what-ifs that have struck their painful blows with more brutality than ever before, I've learned that keeping a grip on the hopeful, joyful what-ifs can soften the blows of the darker ones.

It isn't easy, and I'll never be perfect at it.

But when I let my thoughts meander through the good things that might happen tomorrow instead of the bad, the weight of the world, my past, and the challenges still to come feel a little less heavy.

and so,

Even though you may not always succeed, always do your best to nourish the what-ifs defined by hope, and not by fear.

because the fruits of tomorrow,

of next year,

of my life,
of my family and friends,
of the stranger I hold the door for in the morning,
of the little moments of love in every day,
are the reasons we have to conquer difficult times of
  today
and persist to see the sunshine of another day.

Sincerely,

Emily

Emily Brigham '21

Emily Brigham is a senior Psychology major, with minors in Data Science and ESS. She will be continuing her education at Auburn University in the fall, to pursue a PhD in Human Development and Family Studies. Emily is from Tiverton, Rhode Island, and as a result of living in a coastal farming town, has unconditional love both for the ocean and for cows. When she isn't studying psychology or at the beach, you can find Emily going on long runs, reading a good mystery novel, or forcing her friends to eat her vegan baking.

Open your aperture

Dear Matt,

I am writing this letter some 20 years after you have graduated from Notre Dame. I will try to be brief... there are so many topics to cover, but overall the five below seem like good words of guidance as you enter your freshman year:

1. **Open your aperture.** Meet as many people as you can and work hard to extend your social community. Do not limit yourself by associating with students who only think and act like you. You will learn later in life that different perspectives, different communication styles, and different personalities are what drive great ideas. There are so many unique and talented people at Notre Dame...meet and learn from as many as you can. Don't just "accept" the vast individuality that is inherent in the ND student body ... seek out and embrace that individuality.

2. **Enjoy your friends**...spend as much time as you can with them. You will be moving your family of five 18 years later and, as part of the usual task of throwing so many things out, you will come across a picture of two close friends, hanging out on your porch on Navarre Street. Both will have unexpectedly passed away well before they were 40. You will say to yourself "man, I wish I could go back to that day..." Own the times you have with your close friends ...listen to them and make sure they know how important they are to you.

3. **Embrace the many challenging moments** you will experience as a new member of the Men's Soccer team... you may not realize it then, but those hard lessons are what prepare you most for the professional world. Literally everything you achieve in your professional career for the next 20 years is due to the team around you. Learn how to collaborate and motivate as much as you can... take time to elevate your teammates and work to improve the team every day.

4. **Go home early!** A wise man once told my girlfriend (now wife) at ND, "... nothing good happens after 2:00 AM ..."; boy was he right. When out on a weekend, try to regularly cut the night short and go home as much as you can — you won't regret it.

5. **Savor the lazy Sundays** and commit to watching Goodfellas, Braveheart and The Godfather at least once per quarter while eating Papa Johns in your dorm room. Soon, with three little children, your movie options take a turn for the worse...Madagascar, Jumanji, or Night at the Museum. While still fun, it just isn't the same.

Enjoy the next four years...there are so many amazing students to meet and teachers to learn from. Make the most of it and embrace every day!

Matt

Matt Zimmer '98

Matt Zimmer graduated from the University of Notre Dame in 1998 and majored in Accounting. Matt began his career at PwC and subsequently entered investment banking by joining Robert W. Baird. Matt later joined William Blair & Company, a global boutique investment bank, and has spent time in Blair's U.S. and European offices. Today,

Matt is a partner at William Blair and is the Global Head of Services and Industrials. Matt and his wife Marny (ND '98) live in Chicago with their three young children, Patrick, Rhett, and Will.

Embrace who you are not despite the labels, but in light of them

Dear Freshman Self,

In your senior year of high school you felt unapologetically ambitious, like no obstacle could deter the predetermined course of success. You were top of your class, a youth group leader, admitted to one of the country's best colleges, and you had just learned to drive a stick shift. Walking onto Notre Dame's campus you will feel confident in your ability to succeed and change the world. But in just the first week, your enthusiasm will begin to fade. You'll face the harsh reality that is a "minority" status. I know you understand a minority status intellectually. You can define it, give examples, analyze the term and the groups characterized by it, sure, but you have yet to live it. Growing up in Los Angeles, "Latina" and "low socioeconomic status" were labels with no tangible significance. You understand your identity consists of your personhood, not these external qualifiers. They are relevant in applications or census data, not your interpersonal relationships. I want to warn you that a different understanding of the term will manifest when you embody it daily.

For example, your classmate in Chemistry lab will prefer to ask a fellow white male student across the room for help before asking you who will be standing next to him. At first, you'll think to yourself, "Maybe they know each other

7

or maybe I just look particularly intimidating today." But after several instances of being overlooked you will begin to wonder why they assume you don't know the answer. Then at Milkshake Mass, the sign of peace won't be offered to you or your friends. Specifically, the boys in front of you will shake everyone else's hand but won't turn around to shake yours. Take the initiative to tap them on the shoulder and extend your hand to them. Do not stand to be overlooked in mass, a space meant to be a place of equality.

But Kathy, don't let this discourage you. Make it a mission to regain the confidence you had in Los Angeles, not despite the labels but in light of them. I want you to embrace the reality of your minority status as evidence that our places in society are not fixed. Do this because your time at Notre Dame will be beautiful even if these small incidences boil your blood.

Father Ted Hesburgh will inspire you and comfort you. You don't know who Father Ted is yet but let me tell you this man was a saint. Not only was he an advocate for social justice, he also cared deeply about the students at Notre Dame, regardless of color or background. In fact, it's because of him that women were admitted to the university. He embodies what Notre Dame stands for and that will inspire you like nothing else.

The friends you make this year will become your second family. You are going through this struggle together, facing similar challenges and similar prejudices. But the faith you have in each other and in God will carry you through any and all adversity.

Believe me, this year you will be angry, frustrated, and overwhelmed, but you will also feel loved and hopeful. The challenges you will face will make you stronger and you will feel excited to learn more about yourself and the world around you in the years to come.

Kathy

Kathy Casillas '20

Kathy Casillas grew up in Los Angeles, CA. During her time at Notre Dame, she pursued Neuroscience and Behavior with a minor in Sociology. After graduating from Notre Dame, Kathy aspires to earn a PhD and conduct interdisciplinary research of human behavior integrating social, cognitive, and neurological levels of analysis.

Be yourself - really! That's It!

Dear Sarah,

Are you sitting down? It's your future self here, and I have some news for you that may come as a shock.

In your years at Notre Dame, you sometimes struggled to be yourself.

I know! You're reading this fresh off your high school days, a confident big fish eager to exit her stifling pond. After 18 self-assured years, it may seem impossible that you'd hit a snag now. At Notre Dame, though, you'll finally swim with fish your own size—and, while that will be thrilling, it will also be challenging.

On this campus, you'll meet people who find honors calculus easy and people whose parents are billionaires with a 'B.' Your first crush will go on to be a Rhodes scholar. The girl down the hall? First-round draft pick in the WNBA. Peers like this are a little intimidating for a public-school kid from Indiana, and at times, it will feel tempting—if not downright required—to change yourself to compete.

Eleven years after our orientation, I have one word of advice for you: Don't.

You are as smart as your honors program classmates, even if they dream of curing cancer and you dream of writing for The Onion. You're as good a person as your fellow Folkheads, even if the retreat that brings them closer to God leaves you feeling unmoved. You belong at Notre Dame—even if you can't find a single mold on campus that fits all of you.

Sarah, I have a secret to share. The moments when you thrived the most in college were those when you were most authentic. In your four years, you'll be best known for your sparkling wit. You'll earn applause in cabarets and musicals; you'll win awards for your columns at the Scholastic. Even your GPA will hit its high point when you learn to take classes that sound fun instead of ones that sound impressive.

I'm proud of who you were at Notre Dame. You stood up for yourself when counselors pushed you to take classes you knew you'd fail, and, after some early fears, you brought your whole self to this university, proving that it's not just for legacy students from fancy prep schools, but that it's also for scholarship students from small towns. You were brilliant, and you were brave.

But if I had to do it over again, I would urge you to dial it up. If writing a thesis isn't working for you, write a novel. If you're in a club you don't like, quit! Notre Dame does not need more aspirants to some imagined ideal of the "perfect student." It needs more students to be exactly who they are. Whether Black or White, gay or straight, first- or fifth-generation, everyone deserves a home at Our Lady's University. And if your radical self-acceptance can help someone else see herself here, you'll have accomplished something far more meaningful than any Latin honor.

You're going to love the pond you just moved into, little fish. Be you without apology, and I promise it will love you back.

Your friend,

Sarah

Sarah Cahalan '14

Sarah Cahalan is a writer, humorist, and native Hoosier. At Notre Dame, she studied in the Glynn Family Honors Program and participated in such groups as the Folk Choir, PEMCo, and the Scholastic staff. She has worked for magazines across the United States and Europe, and in 2020, she earned her master's degree from the Medill School of Journalism. She currently lives in Chicago and works for the New York Times.

Growing into Your Authentic Self

Dear Elizabeth,

I know the last six months haven't exactly panned out the way you initially wanted. Your graduation was no longer a magnum opus for the culmination of high school, but rather, a digital slideshow you watched from your sofa. You didn't get to wear that prom dress, or even say goodbye to some of your friends before they went on their separate paths. Despite all those things, I know you're excited to experience Notre Dame.

There's this spot on the lake that has a natural alcove to sit, and mom and I say it's our spot. You're going to discover this spot during move-in, and sometimes, you'll go back to it when you're stressed and just want to feel her presence.

While the first month of college will feel like summer camp,—getting to know new people and experiencing a changed environment, school will suddenly get a bit difficult. You'll realize that you haven't gotten magically better at calculus since high school, and that it's okay to admit you need help. You'll start to get homesick, especially after spending a month listening to cicadas. You'll crave the drizzle of the Pacific Northwest, and during the first rainfall on campus, you'll put on your coat and nearly dance while the rest run for cover. Being from the West Coast is going to become half of your personality trait.

You'll go to Mass for the first time, and you'll be grateful for the masks so that they cover your lips, which don't know the proper responses. However, you'll start to learn , and explore traditions that differ from your own.

Suddenly, you'll find yourself at a vigil, commemorating the lives of two students who were the same age as yourself. You'll join hundreds of students on an empty Saturday night and place a candle at the grotto. You'll find a community of loving individuals, coming together by unfortunate circumstances, but uniting with purpose. You'll finally begin to understand how special Notre Dame is.

Notre Dame isn't merely a university, but rather, a place where you'll learn to grow into your authentic self. That progress doesn't come without practice; you'll find yourself wondering if you belong, and whether you are good enough.

In one stressful study session, you will be in tears huddled over a desk, feeling like you'll never amount to anything. But someone will approach—a complete stranger. They will ask if you are alright, and offer a treat they bought for themselves. It is these people you encounter that will make you realize that you are right where you are supposed to be.

Freshman year will quickly dissipate, and you'll find yourself wondering where the time went. Hold on to those moments, because you'll be where I am now very shortly. I hope you're proud of the person you've become. I think you'll be surprised—in a good way.

Elizabeth Prater

Elizabeth Prater '24

Elizabeth is an undergraduate student at the University of Notre Dame, but she is originally from Vancouver, Washington. She studies marketing and the Program of Liberal Studies. On campus, she writes for The Observer, and plays violin for the Notre Dame Symphony Orchestra. Additionally, she's partaken in projects such as the Dublin Global Gateway Playwriting Workshop, as well as campaigns in Student International Business Council. Elizabeth hopes to bring joy to people through her writing and story-telling abilities.

Commit yourself to learning
for the sake of learning

Dear Freshman Claire,

Four years. That's the amount of precious time you get to call yourself a Notre Dame student. Count yourself lucky, drink up every second that you have, and take full advantage of every opportunity that comes your way.

It's easy for me to selectively forget how hard the transition is to a new academic and social environment (I've now done it twice in the past four years because you're fortunate enough to study abroad!), I've included a few words of advice that I've learned, often through trial and error, about life generally and Notre Dame specifically:

Practice more introspection, about the big things especially. I found that it was easy to go through the motions, to follow an even course by playing it safe. Why are you studying engineering? How will your Notre Dame education (which also extends beyond the classroom) contribute to your goals in life? Are you happy with how you spend your time and the people you share your time with? To be frank, I still don't have fully developed answers to these heavy questions but thinking about them can nevertheless be fruitful. And if you find that you are unsatisfied with the answers you ascertain, take a risk and change something.

Actively engage in the various communities to which you belong - Notre Dame, McGlinn, and South Bend. Apathy is a gateway to laziness and ignorance. Plus, you will meet such a diverse (in all senses of the word) group of friends.

Find passions separate from your circumstances and make time for them no matter where you are. Discover something you love to do irrespective of your studies and your friends, something that will feasibly entertain you through retirement! For example, I found that I love to go on long walks when the weather is beautiful - something that I took advantage of around the lakes here at Notre Dame, through the historic streets and scenic parks around Oxford, and along the Charles River in Boston.

The view that your time here at Notre Dame is only a vehicle to grad school or a lucrative job is frankly superficial (although, inevitably and thankfully, you will have a job at a wonderful company). I can't emphasize enough how important it is to commit yourself to learning for the sake of learning. I know it's hard, given the system of evaluation and examination, but staying curious and thirsty for knowledge, I've discovered at this point in my life, both makes me happy and a more effective learner. Part of the reason that it is so easy to fall into a routine of tailoring your studying toward a specific exam is your fear of failure. Failure is ok!! You will fail (Calculus III final exam, I'm looking at you), you will get problems incorrect, you will be frustrated and annoyed by the fact that you can't, for the life of you, comprehend the implications of Schrodinger's equation, but

DO NOT take the easy way out and give up. You will grow from your failures and mistakes; your friends will still love you, you will still be able to study abroad, and you will manage to get a great job after graduation.

Through all the time you toil in the section lounge or at your desk, make sure to take enough time and effort for self-care. I know it's easier said than done, but too much fro-yo and not enough sleep does not make a happy Claire. Your mental and physical well-being is more important than any assignment or exam.

Do not get trapped under the Notre Dame bubble; we are vulnerable to slide into this mindset, but there are simple patterns of behavior that inspire a general awareness of the world around you. Read the news and discuss current events and philosophical dilemmas with your friends… it's really not hard to do and you don't need to physically leave the bubble in order to do it.

To part, on a somewhat ironic note, don't let anyone else shape your expectations or definition of the "Notre Dame experience." Your experience is uniquely yours – you will have times of jubilation and celebration and sadness and disappointment; late nights studying and late nights socializing. You will meet friends that I hope to know for the rest of my life, fantastically talented, wickedly smart, and incredibly hilarious friends.

As I write this letter, only a few months from graduation, I look back on my time here at Notre Dame dearly; although I feel excited and prepared for the "real world," there is an undeniable part of me that would be lying if I didn't say that I will be very sad to dress in my cap and gown and receive that gilded Notre Dame diploma. Your admission letter warmly stated, "Welcome Home," and as a senior about to fly the nest, I can truly say that this place and these people are truly my home.

Love,

Senior Claire

Claire Gaffney '18

Claire is a senior Electrical Engineering major from Alexandria, VA. She lived in McGlinn Hall where she made best friends and study partners alike. After graduation, she plans to move to Chicago to work at Deloitte.

You cannot make it alone

Dear Kendrick,

You cannot make it alone.

In high school, you were the "cross-country and track team captain, literary aficionado, trombone prodigy and honor society president" that everyone around you epitomized. You dated the "prettiest girls" and competed in the largest competitions any of your classmates had ever seen. From persevering through the trials and tribulations you experienced, you understandably believed you could handle anything single handedly. After all, even though there is no "I" in "team", your team is hundreds of miles away in Las Vegas. Yet even without a team right there with you, I'm sure you believe confidence and intelligence will be more than enough to carry you through your academic career at Notre Dame.

You're wrong.

For as you soon may realize, the University of Notre Dame is not full of the short sighted, degrading fanatics that ostracized you from across the street in high school. This University has collected track stars, book lovers, music prodigies, and honor society students from around the world, all with unique experiences and personas that you will come to love. The only exception is that these students, who will face many of the same challenges you will, do not have to face them with an additional elective on their course load.

This elective course will in fact take many of hours of your life, keeping you awake on exam days and troubling you on weekends. It is not required for your major, nor will it help you achieve course completion in either of your double minors, but it will by far be the biggest inhibitor to success. You will need a team to help you get through it and every second you wait will hurt you in more ways than one.

For "Pretending to not be Gay" is a five-credit course and you're overloaded.

It is going to hurt, and you're going to suffer, but looking back you will finally realize how foolish you were to believe your Notre Dame friends wouldn't accept you. From the boy you hit with your trombone during the final "Band of the Fighting Irish" marching audition, to the girl who will teach you why liturgical choir music is some of the most beautiful in the world, you will form a team. This team will help you realize that a five-credit course in not being yourself is not only dumb but "high key unnecessary." You will grow strong alongside them and they will become your roommates, counselors, leaders and friends. Soon you will not only lead an organization that assists those like you, but recruit hundreds through your executive admissions role. Finally, you will stand in front of the class of 2021, your band directors and your peers and give them an induction speech of a lifetime.

You will not make it through your first year at Notre Dame alone, and I promise with the phenomenal family you meet here, you won't have to.

Kendrick

Kendrick Peterson '20

Kendrick Peterson is currently an undergraduate student from Las Vegas, Nevada, at the University of Notre Dame. In addition to living in St. Edwards Hall, he has a wide variety of commitments ranging from performing trombone in ensembles like the marching band to competing on the club cross country team. His primary major is Political Science, however with minors in Business Economics and Public policy he definitely remains busy. In addition, he also sits as an acting officer and the Alumni outreach student representative of Prism ND (the LGBTQ+ Human rights organization on campus). All of his many roles on campus have blessed him with the opportunity to truly make an impact, and hopefully over time he can become someone who encourages many others to do the same.

Welcome home

To my freshman year self,

Welcome home! You are about to embark on a four-year journey that will forever change your life. You may not realize this now, but after four years it will be hard to imagine that you ever thought of going anywhere else.

Notre Dame is a really amazing place, as you're about to find out. You may feel scared and a little alone right now —know that you're not the only one feeling like this. This feeling will seem crazy to you in four years when you're crying with your friends on graduation night, wondering where the time went and wishing you could do it all over again. When that day comes (and it's going to come faster than you think!), make sure you have no regrets. Notre Dame has so much to give you, so take every little thing that you can.

Before you left for college, Mom shared some life advice with you. She said, "Only half of what you will learn in college will be in the classroom." Don't forget this. You're about to spend four years surrounded by some of the smartest and most hardworking people in the country. It's easy to feel as if you should spend every waking moment studying, especially during those times when you're really struggling and wondering if you're actually smart enough to be here. Remember to take a step back and appreciate your life and the people in it. Is staying up with your friends talking until

23

3 AM when you should be doing your homework a good choice? Well, you may be a little tired the next day, but I promise you—you will still pass that class, and it's not the nights you spent studying alone that you're going to remember in 10 years. Your professors have so much to teach you, but don't discount the lessons that you'll learn from other people in your life—whether it's a mentor, your best friend, or someone in front of you in the Starbucks line.

The words 'Welcome home!' may seem like a cheesy line that someone in the Admissions Office came up with to recruit students. You walk into your dorm room on move-in day, greeted by an extremely enthusiastic Welcome Weekend staff, and meet your new roommate for the first time. You make your way through your first week of classes, wondering how you're going to possibly have time to finish your homework. You cheer in the stands on Game Day, eat lunch in the dining hall, take a few trips to the Grotto. And slowly but surely, you start to realize that Notre Dame is more than just a school. You finally understand what everyone means when they call it home.

Before you know it, you'll be hugging your friends on graduation night, wondering how you will possibly live without these people that have become your family in this place you now call home. So, don't blink, and make sure to enjoy every second.

Alyson

Alyson Duzansky '17
Alyson Duzansky is a Class of 2017 graduate. She graduated with a degree in Chemical Engineering and was an active member of the Society of Women Engineers. She is currently living in Washington, D.C. and working for Accenture as a Technology Consultant.

Simply Lesson
Written Anonymously

Hey freshman me,

Before all else, I want you to know that you belong here. You belong at the University of Notre Dame in every way imaginable, and there is nothing you can ever do to change that. Do not believe the lie that you are not good enough because you are more than good enough. God has put you here for a reason, and He will not bring you here just to leave. He's with you in the highs and He's with you in the lows. Trust in Him. I promise He will never let you down. He has your back in more ways than you can possibly imagine. Finally, trust in His word because He will prove time and time again that it is true.

Let me give you some advice that will save you a lot of heartache. For one, don't overthink. It's so easy to do, but it isn't helpful. I know you think that the best way to get to the root of a problem is to think of it constantly until it's removed; however, by overthinking, you're just deepening it. It only leads to damage, not strength, and it causes you to consider the worst scenarios that won't even take place. There is a reason why God tells you not to worry. He has everything worked out, and trust me, it's better than any story you could write.

Your worth is not in what you do. It's not in sports,

clubs, grades, or anything else. Your worth is completely set in Jesus, and you are loved like nobody's business. There's nothing you can do to change your worth or how much God loves you, so don't spend hours thinking about how it could change. You don't crinkle up a dollar bill and see its value diminish. It's the same with you. Thinking that what you do can impact your worth is ridiculous and untrue. All it does is steal your joy.

Believe in yourself! You completely deserve to. Remember that how you view yourself is more important than how others view you. You control your thoughts. You decide what you believe, so believe in things that make you stronger. God believes in you and He knows you better than you know yourself, so why doubt yourself?

Promise me that you will enjoy your first year of college. Promise me you will not worry or overthink because doing so just steals from your joy–it's pointless. . God is writing your story, so do not worry. He will set everything in its place. Remember that I love you, and I believe in you with my whole being. Believe in yourself and trust in God.

Love,
Future you

Don't quit, give yourself time to adjust

Dear Bob,

If you met me these days, you'd probably think I bleed blue and gold. And that'd be a fair assumption. I recently served on Notre Dame's board of trustees and I now serve on the Keough School's advisory council. I enjoy coming back for football games and I'm part of a long family legacy at the university. My mother, a Notre Dame Law School graduate, is even named Dillon, since one of her great-great uncles was Rev. Patrick Dillon, C.S.C., president of Notre Dame during the Civil War.

It's a perfect Notre Dame story.

But during my first semester, I almost left.

It was tough. After being a star student at a big public high school near Philadelphia, I found myself lost among countless stars in Indiana. It was hard to make friends. My cramped room at Zahm seemed to be designed for one person, yet I had two roommates, both with wildly different schedules. My twin brother James hadn't been accepted to Notre Dame, leaving me miffed about the place from the start. Looking for something to do, I sought out a reporting job at The Observer, but it didn't click.

As the humdrum 2004 football season dragged on—

the Irish went 6-6 in Ty Willingham's final season—I began to think about transferring. Notre Dame was phony, I told myself, and I might as well head back to Pennsylvania and be with people I liked, maybe at Temple University or Penn State. I felt surrounded by well-dressed, good-looking and athletic students from around the country who were fitting in just fine and loving every minute. Meanwhile, I sat in the computer lab in the student center most nights in a hoodie, clicking through political news and listening to the Dave Matthews Band.

On the phone with my parents one night, they said they'd support me if I left Notre Dame, but urged me not to leave too abruptly. They told me to think it through and try to enjoy college a little more, to be less grouchy and less tense. I reluctantly agreed and shelved the transfer applications. Throughout the rest of my freshman year, I slogged on, slowly appreciating my classes and the people I met.

An epiphany or some magic moment where I suddenly fell in love with Notre Dame on a walk by the lakes as I listened to the "Rudy" soundtrack never came. There was simply that quiet decision on a winter evening to not quit. But that was everything. By choosing to stay, I challenged myself to adapt and change, to plow through small grievances and many mistakes and to keep on, to be a man.

It paid off: my brother James eventually transferred in and we both majored in American Studies. During senior year, we lived in Dillon Hall and he was my resident assistant. My sister Ellen was a freshman at Notre Dame by then and lived across South quad. I ended up interviewing Dave Matthews for The Observer. Rev. John Jenkins, C.S.C., became a friend and mentor along the way.

My advice to you: don't quit. Freshman year isn't easy, and Notre Dame isn't perfect. But give it time. Give yourself time.

Robert Costa '08

Robert Costa is a national political reporter for the Washington Post, moderator of PBS's "Washington Week," and a political analyst for NBC News and MSNBC. He covers the White House and Congress, and frequently appears on "Meet the Press" and "Morning Joe." Washingtonian magazine has said he is "one of the next generation of journalists worth following." He is a 2008 graduate of the University of Notre Dame and earned a master's degree in politics in 2009 from the University of Cambridge, where he studied Winston Churchill.

Embrace your identity, keep an open mind

Dear Freshman Stacey,

As your plane takes off for the Bend in time for Welcome Weekend, you gaze down at the city you've called home for the past 18 years. You are oddly reminded of the memory of tossing your graduation cap at Carnegie Hall - a day of nicely done hair, heels, hugs, photoshoots, and proud parents. You fell in love with this campus from your first visit a few months ago and hope to fall in love with the people as well. Not a single one of the 850 students from your graduating high school class will attend Notre Dame, but your heart still beats with excitement to reunite with the gorgeous campus, start on a clean slate, and make new friends.

Stacey, this school year will be filled with unexpected twists and turns, exciting first-timers, and a whole mix of emotions. You will discover new sports like spikeball and cornhole, tailgate for the first time, and watch your first game in the stadium instead of on the screen. Growing up with and coming from a high school with mostly Asian-Americans, you will find the community at Notre Dame much different from home. It's okay to miss your parents' homemade meals and authentic Asian food that South Bend lacks. It's okay to prefer to watch c-dramas and k-dramas over The Bachelorette. Let your differences allow you to stand out from the crowd, enlighten others about your culture, and create a strong sense of pride for your unique identity. Get involved in the cultural clubs on campus filled with people who bring the comforts of home, relatable stories, and cultural bonding. At the same time, let Notre Dame be the place to branch into a new world and meet different people. Keep an open mind and try new things. Exchange your stories with the people you meet and share the best experiences and memories with them in college.

Along with a huge transition from home to college 700 miles away, be prepared for a year and a world of drastic changes. The unexpected pandemic will lead to cancelled plans with friends from home and a freshman year abruptly cut short. Make the most of your time on campus and stay connected with your loved ones. In a world of social distancing and remote learning, the joy and excitement that comes from late movie nights with friends, weekend parties, maskless workouts, and dining hall dates is lost. Looking back, I definitely would've cherished the pre-pandemic times on campus even more. Spending the rest of your school year via Zoom and only being able to see your friends through FaceTime will be rough, so make sure to take care of your well-being, check in on friends and family often, and find ways to stay active at home.

Your first year at Notre Dame will definitely be an interesting one, and I am so excited for you! Make the most out of your time with your friends and be open to the exciting opportunities that you encounter throughout your college journey.

Much love and many prayers,

Stacey

Stacey Xue '23

Stacey is a resident of Johnson Family Hall originally from New York City studying accounting and applied mathematics. At Notre Dame, Stacey serves as treasurer of Asian American Association, accounting director of the Student International Business Council, vice president of Asian Business Society, and social media coordinator of the Red Cross Club. She works part-time with The Observer and plays flute in the symphonic band. In her free time, she enjoys composing classical music, watching football, playing chess, running cross country, and traveling around the world whenever possible.

It's About More Than What You Feel

Written Anonymously

I guess one could say that I had the "ultimate" first year college experience. Despite a global pandemic, I made relationships that I never want to fade away, I never had a weekend that wasn't a blast, my grades are fine, and my extremely indecisive self even figured out what I want to study. And yet, as I reflect on this past year, I must admit it was not all great.

For so many days, I felt unaccomplished, worthless, and worst of all, so alone.

In regard to feeling unaccomplished, for so many days this past year I felt like I was never doing enough. I was successful both inside and outside the classroom, and yet I was never satisfied with myself.

Notre Dame has felt like home since the moment I first stepped foot on this campus, and yet, for so many days I felt like I was not worthy of calling somewhere so beautiful, home.

Despite being surrounded by people that I felt lucky to know, I often ended each day feeling so detached and lonely. I wish I allowed myself to venture for help when I first started feeling such negativity. But, instead, I replayed in my head all the positive things other had to say about me:

"You're the happiest person I know."

"You can brighten anyone's day."

"I don't think anyone can hate you, your heart is too big."

Though I appreciated hearing such kind words about me, they always seemed hollow and irrelevant.

It wasn't until my second semester that I finally realized I needed to tell someone. Trust me, I did not want to open up to anyone. I enjoyed the way I was, confiding to my diary and conversing loudly with the universe every night before bed. But I could no longer handle feeling so low, and as my fear of asking for help faded, I found the strength to confide in someone.

My issues were not settled by a simple conversation. However, there was comfort in being able to share that I felt unaccomplished, and this vulnerability allowed me to see all that I had achieved. It was soothing to tell someone I felt worthless, and they reminded me that I am in fact deserving. And it was beautiful to tell someone I felt alone, and they had me list everyone I am so grateful to have.

I guess this letter wasn't addressed specifically to my freshman year self, nor was it really addressed to anyone. I hope that if you've read it in its entirety, you'll understand that your feelings are valid, and you're allowed to have doubts even in good times. Life is beautiful, and when it brings you pain, you work to heal. It always gets so much better when you do.

Listen more, ask more, worry less

Dear Erin,

Listen more. Ask more. Worry less.

Listen more. You are surrounded by classmates who traveled from across the world, hold different views, bring varied cultural traditions, have unique talents, and display a range of economic backgrounds. You grew up in a small Wisconsin farming town of 1,200 where you knew most of your classmates from kindergarten through senior year. You visited only Chicago, Disney World, and Washington DC before coming to Notre Dame. Take more time to listen to the stories of those who will share the next four years with you. Living together in a community of randomly assigned residents is something unique to ND and offers an opportunity that you will never again be able to replicate. Do not take Siegfried women too much for granted while you are off concentrating on the next test or working in student government. Someday, the stories of people may be what you remember most.

Ask more. Rectors, professors, priests in residence, choir directors, club advisors, and administrators are not authority figures to pass in the hallway with a brief hello or consult only in times of need. No, you are not bothering Sr. Mo by stopping to talk. Professor Kaplan really meant that he hoped students would keep in touch. The seemingly straight path to majoring in accounting, a Big 8 summer internship, and an audit or tax job might not actually be right for you. Pause and ask yourself which classes you like best and why. Ask if there are other career options much earlier. Discuss your answers to these questions with those who have wisdom beyond your years. In other words, do not just follow a script because you think that it is the only way to get your student loans paid off. Years later, you will realize that professors, rectors, and even Student Affairs VPs have chosen to work at a University precisely to support your formation and assist in your discernment. They do not find talking to students an inconvenience. And Father Jenkins, one of the three professors you actually had the courage to talk with at office hours, might one day remember you and offer you an amazing job at your alma mater!

Worry less. Even with these tweaks, take heart. Some things you will actually get right the first time. It will take time to meet friends, but once you find them, they last. Melanie, Shaun, Sean, Brandon, Ed, Tracy and Stacy will be part of your life for decades. Laugh often. Stay up late. Savor the beauty of campus, especially at night or as the seasons change. Get free popcorn at the Oak Room, and do not be too sad when it closes to renovate South Dining Hall. Pray often at Siegfried and Zahm Hall Masses. Sing in Lit Choir (stop rolling your eyes, you grow to love it). Work hard. Take that lucky call from McKinsey. Try to be a servant leader. Know that the moment when ND will feel like home will come more quickly than you think in those first few scary and lonely months. Thank your Mom & Dad for the amazing opportunity and sacrifices they made so you could attend this special place. Have patience. Trust.

Open yourself to growing in both mind and heart. And dating your friend Ryan will turn out well.

With love,
Older you, who would do it all again in a heartbeat

Erin Hoffman Harding '97

Erin Hoffmann Harding served as Vice President for Student Affairs from 2012 to 2021. As Vice President for Student Affairs Ms. Hoffmann Harding oversaw five areas comprised of multiple departments related to residential life, student development, student services, campus ministry, and career and professional development. She previously served as associate vice president for strategic planning and special projects. Prior to coming to Notre Dame in 2005, Ms. Hoffmann Harding served as a management consultant in the Chicago and Cleveland offices of the international consulting firm McKinsey and Company Inc. She is a summa cum laude graduate of Notre Dame's Mendoza College of Business and earned her juris doctor degree magna cum laude from Harvard Law School. She and her husband, Ryan, also a Notre Dame graduate and an attorney, are the parents of three young sons.

Glass half full

Dear freshman self,

Your time at Notre Dame is going to be unprecedented.

You'll spend three and a half years looking forward to senior year, creating bucket lists for all of the things you want to do, and secretly hoping that your last year will outshine the other three exponentially.

But all of that will change with one email.

So live life now. Do not save it for next year nor for your last year. Do the things that you want to do now. Participate in the Notre Dame traditions now. Make new friends now. Ask that question in class now. Go to that event now. Learn how to be okay with making a fool out of yourself now. Stop waiting for a future that's going to be better than the now - make the now better.

Honestly, in the years between now and your senior year, you won't live up to the great expectations you have for yourself. You'll fall short academically, socially, spiritually, and so on. Nobody in the world could have predicted that we'd be living in a global pandemic in what was supposed to be the best year of your life thus far according to your plans. Everything will feel like a waste.

But life isn't ever going to be how you expect it to be. You shouldn't linger in all of your disappointment and regret. These times are unprecedented and losing out on normality is disappointing, but holding onto that sadness detracts from all the goodness that is still present all around you. That is not the way to spend the time you have left at one of the greatest places in the world. Living in fear and anger and sadness won't make the pandemic go away.

There's still going to be tears. There's still going to be anger. There's going to be frustration and intense sadness. There's going to be loneliness. There's even going to be a couple days when you can barely manage to get out of bed to go to online class because you didn't come all the way to Notre Dame for online class.

But there's also so much goodness to be found this year.

You'll deepen your friendships even further. You'll fall in love with your major over and over again. You'll find joy and laughter amid the chaos. You will grow closer to God again. You'll choose a path for post-grad. You'll experience intense happiness. You'll be excited for the small things. You will relish every single moment that it will feel like it's a normal, good year.

So, my advice: spend time outside. Get creative when it comes to socializing in the midst of a pandemic. Keep open lines of communication with your parents for encouragement, with your friends to check up on (and to have people to check up on you), with your professors to ask for more extensions this year than you have in the last three years combined. Tell others about your frustrations, and listen to theirs. Reach out to your rector because she has a big, big heart. And, for heaven's sake, have mercy on yourself and everyone else as we all try to navigate these unprecedented times.

Your life at Notre Dame is not going to play out like you expected it to, but it will be so, so good.

Always in Notre Dame,

Kenzie

Kenzie Hengesbach '21

Kenzie is from a small town in rural mid-Michigan, and she came to Notre Dame in the footsteps of her older sister. She is a first-generation student who spent her four years at Notre Dame searching for a life to be passionate about, which she found in her studies of psychology and theology. Her favorite thing to do in her free time at Notre Dame was to attend daily Mass in the basilica, and her biggest regret is not finishing the chapel crawl that Kenzie and her best friend had planned out. She also enjoys being with friends, good weather, and eating Ben & Jerry's Milk and Cookies ice cream from the Huddle. After graduation, she will be returning to mid-Michigan and joining Michigan State University's College of Education to pursue an Educational Specialist degree in School Psychology.

Like a wave

Larissa,

I hope when you read this letter, you're the happiest you've ever been. I hope you're still feeling the elation of being accepted to the University of Notre Dame. This feeling will never completely go away, but it will evolve. When you're on campus, it will come over you like a wave, pushing you towards your goals and pulling you back into yourself.

Embrace it. Enjoy it. Remember that feeling.

You've been pulled out of your comfort zone, away from everything and everyone you know, and transplanted into the middle of the Midwest. It's equally exciting and frightening. Your bravery and passion will get you through those tough moments: late night studying, disagreeing with friends, missing your family, and feeling like you're not on the right path. Here I say - don't be afraid to really know and be yourself.

Trust your intuition. Build awareness of your emotions, limits, and strength.

You will be surrounded by astounding young scholars, mentors, professors, roommates, and friends. Each of them will bring something new into your life. They will introduce you to new people, music, art, and so many other wonderful topics. Likewise, you will introduce them to your Diné heritage, culture, and language. Many of these people will remain close friends, and others will depart in their own direction. Appreciate their presence, the moments you have with them, and the memories you create together.

Learn what it means to value, and also to protect your relationships.

Shiyázhí, there are so many challenging lessons you will experience and learn during your time at Notre Dame. Sometimes, the distress of your hardships will overtake you, and when this happens, know that you are not alone. Don't be afraid to ask for help when you need it, and most of all, don't be afraid to stop, breathe, and take a break. You are a strong, resilient Diné woman, but you are not invincible. In these difficult moments, look to your traditional Diné beliefs to strengthen your faith. Remember the words of nimásání: "Never say you feel alone or that you don't have a home." Nimásání would say this in reference to your home on the Navajo Nation, but you will soon realize that she was also talking about the University of Notre Dame.

Recognize the power you carry as a Diné woman.

Your academic journey at Notre Dame will not be like everyone else's and that's what makes your journey so amazing and special. Sometimes, you'll feel like you don't belong but fight that feeling. Remind yourself that you earned the right to call yourself a Notre Dame student and that nobody can take that away— not even you.

Larissa, you have always been your own toughest critic, but your spirit is also more resilient than you know. Nurture yourself and your spirit with love, care, and compassion. There, you will find the light you seek, and there, you will realize that you are capable of anything.

Stay strong Little One.

Larissa Nez '19

Larissa is a Diné citizen, academic, writer, youth advocate, cultural critic, and curator. She is of the Mud People and born for the Mountain Cove People. Her maternal grandfather is of the Red Running Into the Water People and her paternal grandfather is of the Big Water People. She was born and raised on the Navajo Nation, in a small community in northern Arizona. Larissa is currently a Master's student in Public Humanities at Brown University. Her multidisciplinary research explores the intersections between Indigenous Studies, Black Studies, and critical theory as they relate to modern and contemporary art practices, public humanities, and the formation of collections and archives. She currently serves as the Communication Director for the Native American Alumni Board of Directors at the University of Notre Dame and is a member of the College Art Association's Student and Emerging Professionals Committee.

Cherish every moment

Dear Aidan,

This letter is for you, as your head hits the pillow and you drift off to sleep in your newly decorated college dorm room after an exhausting, yet exciting, Welcome Weekend. For you, as you are flung into the air and your stomach drops for that brief moment that you are weightless—your first touchdown push-ups, Irish fans roaring around you, energy electric in the stadium. For you, as you try on costumes and dresses with your roommates for your first SYR in the tent behind McGlinn and your first formal in LaFun Ballroom, jittery with nerves and excitement. For you, as you slip your California-born feet into your first-ever pair of winter boots, spinning through the fresh snow that has draped campus in a muted white blanket, face fixed in an unbreakable smile. For you, as you march defiantly across campus alongside your best friends from McGlinn Hall to your first Organic Chemistry exam in Stepan Center, frosty February morning air biting at your fingers as they clutch firmly to your review sheet, Eye of the Tiger splintering the 7am silence. This letter is for you, from me, two weeks after I've graduated from the University of Notre Dame.

If I could tell you two things about your time at ND, here's what I'd share—embrace the uncomfortable, and invest in people. Many things in college will feel new. Living away from home, spending twenty-four hours a day with friends and roommates, learning how you study best, discovering how to engage in meaningful self-care, and discerning your next steps after graduation—none of this is easy, and there will be times that you struggle with balance. College is a period of transition, and that is unfamiliar and uncomfortable by nature. The pandemic sending a rift through your college education just past the midway point didn't make things any easier, and there will be times that nothing feels like it's going right. These are the precise times when you should pause and reflect. Rest is productive, even though it may seem counterintuitive. Listen to what your mind, body, and heart are telling you—it's okay not to be okay. Lean on others as you embrace the uncomfortable—trust me, I'm on the other side of it now. It might be uncomfortable to say no to a night out with friends and honor your need for rest, or to be one of only two freshmen on a Global Medical Brigade to Nicaragua, or to randomly sign up for a Social Concerns Seminar over winter break. However, each of these uncomfortable choices—whether in the name of exploring your passions or prioritizing your well-being—is how you will flourish. You will become a version of yourself who you may never have expected, and who you are proud to be.

The best part is that you are never alone in these moments of discomfort. Notre Dame is home to people who are not only driven, intelligent, insightful, and passionate, but who are also genuine, kind, loyal, and down-to-earth. Even when they may seem like they have it all together, there are times when they lose their way, too. As cliche as it sounds, Notre Dame's mission to educate both the mind and heart rings true. The commitment of Notre Dame students to be a force for good in the world brings together a pretty phenomenal group of people, let me tell you. Seize every moment with them while you have it—invest in people. Spend time with people from your dorm, from classes, from clubs, from seminars, from student government, from intramural sports—all corners of campus. By the time you graduate, you will look back and realize that you have found a family who will support you no matter where in the world you end up, for the rest of your life.

So, this letter is for you. As your head hits the pillow, as you're thrown into the air, as you get ready for dances, as you lace up your winter boots, and as you march across campus with the best friends of your life, cherish every moment. I'd do anything to be back in your shoes and have these four years ahead of me again. Go get 'em.

Love,

Aidan

Aidan Crowley '21

Aidan Crowley graduated summa cum laude from the University of Notre Dame in 2021 with a major in Neuroscience & Behavior and minors in Poverty Studies and Compassionate Care in Medicine. This fall, she will begin a dual MD/JD program at the University of Pennsylvania Perelman School of Medicine on a full-tuition merit scholarship. During her time at Notre Dame, she was involved in several Center for Social Concerns seminars, conducted medical ethics research at Mayo Clinic, spent a semester in Copenhagen, Denmark, and wrote her senior thesis on mental and emotional performance of physicians during COVID-19 in collaboration with the Center for Compassionate Care in Medicine. Aidan plans to pursue a career at the intersection of clinical medicine, medical ethics, and national healthcare policy reform. In addition to her research involvements, Aidan enjoyed playing on the club tennis team, serving as Editor of Student Life & Athletics for The Dome Yearbook, giving campus tours for the Office of Undergraduate Admissions, and spending time with friends at Notre Dame football games.

Challenge your beliefs, Then do it again
Written Anonymously

To you,

I am absolutely sure that in four years, I will have no idea who you are. And I think that's a good thing. It seems wrong to aspire to lose you, my former self. But this time is exactly when and where it's supposed to happen: in college, when you're expected to discover who you are and have it all figured out in four brief years. After all, you are socially independent but financially dependent- the one time in your life where things will be this way in this wonderful, exploratory realm of finding "you."

They say that this is the time to discover yourself, but how exactly do you do that? Especially during a pandemic where it's difficult to make genuine connections in the first place. It seems like everyone is putting on a mask (figuratively and literally) just to keep a friend they don't even really vibe with, but at least it's someone, and they cling on so they don't feel so alone.

With that being said, I hope you never pretend to be someone you're not even if it means you get to hang with the "popular" crowd. In four years, I'm sure you will look back on your time at Notre Dame and remember the people that made you feel good about being you, rather than that one Friday night you got invited to the football house

47

and spent the night losing yourself. We live in a world that preaches conformity. I hope you defy that.

This is the time to challenge yourself, to question why you believe what you do, and to do it again and again and again. You grew up in a place that told you only one way of thinking worked. Uniformity is ignorantly comfortable. Change is brilliantly terrifying. And borrowed beliefs aren't real. I hope you challenge every single thing you think you believe. Listen to other's viewpoints respectfully. Convey your own ideas to them. Try to find common ground in a time where as a nation and as a campus we appear more divided than ever, because honestly, we have more in common as human beings than the lines we scream from would make you believe. I hope above all else that you come out of college as a better person, ready to be that force for good in the world that you were instilled to be from the moment you signed that contract that made you a part of the Notre Dame family.

For now, just take it one day at a time. Don't rush it, because these four years will go by faster than you could ever imagine, and they'll be the same four years in which you end up making the best memories. Live in the moment, because these moments are the ones you will always wish could last forever when you look back.

But for now, I hope you look forward.

Fresh air from beyond the bubble

Hi, hi, hiiiiiiiiiii!!!!!!!!!

Sometimes it's hard to breathe in the bubble, so here's a bit of fresh air: Other people will try to impose what they think is right on you, but you're the only one who has to live it every day. Let go of the list of "shoulds" and figure it out for yourself!

You're a reflective sort, Shannon. You're also the queen of lists, checking boxes, and people-pleasing. Yup, I know you. I am you. And despite all of the wet noodling, you're still you. Even when you don't know who you are, don't know where you belong, and feel like you've lost your soul, you're still you. So, here's a little insight from the future and a friendly reminder to be who YOU are.

Your favorite spot on campus is the path between the trees just past the lakes that gives a lesson in life perspective. All of the trees seem random until you step forward, look back, and see they fall into perfect rows. Sometimes things don't make sense in the moment but when you reflect on the past, you can see how they were building and preparing you for what came next.

You have a vision for where you are and who you are 10 years from now. But, I'll spare you the drama and cut to the chase, you won't be there. I get the desire to get things figured out, locked in, and settle down. But, that's not how things will unfold. Life doesn't happen that way. You can tell God your plan but he's got abs of steel from laughing so hard every time you do. So, set yourself free from the script and model that doesn't fit. You'll change your major 5 times and your career journey will look a little chaotic to an outside observer but, like the trees on the path, each step will prepare you uniquely and specifically for what's ahead. And, in many ways, very differently and more robustly than you could have ever imagined! Sometimes it's hard to see that in the moment but you're building the muscles to trust in that a bit more and will continue to be surprised and amazed by what unfolds. Enjoy it!!

You'll have A LOT of conversations about values, criteria, and intentions throughout the next four years, and then the four after that, and well, I think you get the point ... forever. You're starting your first semester but when you're starting your last semester, your dad will have a line for you: "when you need a sign, there will be one." Trust the process. Keep going.

Crazy enough, in 10 years, you'll be working with a friend you meet as tutors in the Writing Center. You'll be on a road trip (with all of your belongings in a 2-door car) that you'll call the "heart tour" because the heart wants what it wants, goes where it wants, and does what it wants. You won't check the boxes you think you'll check by that point but whose list is it anyways? Revise the list. Seek feelings of home, peace, and being you. Settle into who YOU are, not who you think other people want or expect you to be. Host a party for one by a party of one.

Between now and 10 years from now, you'll pack up your belongings and move every year. It's easy to get lost in the weeds (or the trees!) of logistical details, but it's the why and the who that really matter. Strive with the same intensity and purpose you do now. Treasure the incredible people who hold your heart. Appreciate all of the connections you make, the conversations that explicitly shift and shape you and the ones that prompt you to process on your own, and all of the opportunities for growth and mentors who develop you.

After graduation, your dad will say a line that sticks with you: "as long as you wake up in the morning, there's something unfinished." As long as we're alive, we're soul searching and discerning. Every moment, day, year, etc. is an opportunity for us to choose something and get closer to who we are meant to become. But sometimes it's really hard to do that when it doesn't seem like there's a model for it. You might get fatigued by the annual soul-searching and life overhaul, but it's mostly because you're trying to bounce between models that don't fit. Square pegs just don't fit into round holes, unless you do A LOT of sanding. So, wade through the turbulence with a glimpse of the light at the end of the tunnel!

I am so excited for your soul searching and can't wait to hear about your revelations and musings along the way! Oh wait, I've already re-read the 500+ pages of the MoSH (Musings of Shannon Hagedorn - a term you'll coin on Jacob's ladder in the gym) and daily gratitude reflections from the past 10 years (that you started before getting baptized freshman year). It's a ride beyond your wildest dreams. Embrace it.

Wishing you the very best and sending oodles of love your way!!!! (please accept at least some of it sooner rather than later)

Shannon

Shannon Hagedorn '15

Shannon Hagedorn is a 2015 grad who majored in Management Consulting and Psychology. On campus, she spent most of her time having long life chats in some form or fashion with her peeps in Pasquerilla West, as a tutor in the Writing Center, or as an intern in the Career Center. Her passion for the career discernment and development processes inspired her to pursue her M. Ed. at Penn State, where she served as the Diversity Programming Coordinator for Career Services. She then returned to Notre Dame to establish the Learning Specialist position in Academic Services for Student-Athletes, applied her change management experience to support large corporate transformations as a consultant at KPMG in New York, found her way back to higher education as a BSBA Career Coach at WashU in St. Louis, and is currently helping organizations uncover the untapped potential of their workforces and empower individuals to maximize their strengths as the Workforce of the Future Product Owner at CFGI! She's been actively involved on the alumni club boards for her various cities and strives to build intentional and inclusive cultures of belonging.

Give of yourself

Dear Christina,

The best four years of your life await you. This time at Notre Dame will go by quickly, but somehow 20 years later will feel like it was just yesterday. You will meet your best friends. You will find yourself. Both will happen, even without you looking. You will carry this time with you for the rest of your life.

Sleep less. Say "yes" more. Repeat those words to remind yourself often. As much as I know now that sleep deeply restores the mind and body (and you will learn to live with less sleep when you have the big family you always dreamed of), try to figure out a way that you are less tied to what you should do and more committed to what you want to do. These memories will last a lifetime, make as many as you can!

Explore. Try new things—join clubs you are interested in even if your friends aren't or take an elective that you are curious about but scared to try. Love your close circle of friends, but know that having different groups of friends will bring new connections for everyone. Grab a meal with your project teammates. Say yes to attend the SYR of someone you might not be interested in. Many years later you will run into these people and be happy for the connection. Stay up all night talking and laughing with your roommates, your time living together is short.

Explore your faith. Just because you didn't grow up a practicing Catholic, use this time to ask questions. Understand the traditions, learn about Mass, then you will know enough to make an educated decision for yourself. Don't be self-conscious, you will come to learn that faith is about values, and you share the same values as many of those around you.

Your life may be hard. You'll question why this is. You will keep a tight eye on the money you earn from your on-campus job, that's all you have. Classes will seem so much harder than in high school. You won't have the family contacts to help you secure internships. But don't discount your greatest qualities which you gained from working hard for what you have. Your friends may seem more mature, more experienced, more worldly, but you should know that they love and admire you for your unique qualities in the same way you look up to them. You may not be able to see this clearly, but you are unique and equal. Thousands of others tried to be one of the lucky freshman at Notre Dame, but there was something extraordinary about you that the University spotted. So, give of yourself. Contribute to the community. Soak in every day, every memory. Be grateful for all you have been given, every single day.

You deserve to be here, and don't forget that. You may come from a blue collar, low income home, most of your friends attend community college, if any college at all, but you worked for this, you can do it, and you deserve it. Everyone has insecurities, even if you don't see them. Don't let that hold you back. Dad always said that with a good education you can make anything for yourself. And you do. Because of Notre Dame, you will be able to become the person you always wanted to be.

Participate in the Notre Dame Family, it's one that will

fulfill you for your entire life. Be proud yet humble of this extraordinary community you are a part of. You will meet many people connected to the University in the years to come, and they will always make you feel welcome.

Your life does not turn out exactly as you had planned, it's not perfect. You made some career decisions and then changed your mind. You regret how you acted in some situations. You do not have the perfect double income family with 2.5 kids and a white picket fence. But the risks you took and the lessons you learned were worth it. You are happy. You are very, very happy. And you have more love in your life than you could have ever imagined. Starting today, every single day state three things you are grateful for, and it will be the key to your happiness.

Life is Good,

Your future self

Christina Glorioso '95, '99

Christina is a single mom for four sons under the age of 6! Christina serves on the Monogram Club Board of Directors, on the Deans Advisory Council of the Mendoza College of Business, and was honored as a "Distinguished Alumni" by Mendoza. After being a Finance undergrad major and working in technology, she went back to ND for her MBA and started her career in Entertainment Marketing. She is currently Senior Vice President of Integrated Marketing at NBCUniversal, overseeing sales marketing for TODAY, Nightly News, Meet the Press, MSNBC and CNBC as well a local small business owner. Prior to starting her family, Christina earned her Master Diver SCUBA certification and has summited Mount Kilimanjaro. But what she loves to do most is mentor hundreds of Notre Dame students and recent graduates over the years.

Expect the worst, hope for the best

Dear freshman self,

Welcome to Notre Dame! You are well aware of how God brought you to this blessed place. You never thought you would be a student at Our Lady's University, but she brought you here according to God's perfect will. Over these next four years, by being true to yourself and not living out someone else's narrative for your life, you will achieve the most growth, foster sincere friendships, and inspire those around you by your life.

Your Notre Dame story will be a unique one by the end of your four years. By following your heart and living out your own story, amazing experiences will ensue. You will enjoy every course in your biology and theology studies, without exception. You may join an environmental research lab because you are fascinated that the seeds of their plant species can germinate into viable sedges even after 100 years of dormancy! Follow this curiosity—it could lead to great contributions to research over the years. You may discover your favorite author during one of your courses, just as I discovered G. K. Chesterton and fell in love with his works. Though you think of yourself as a reserved person, you may live in a "sixman" room for three years in your dorm. You may be surprised at how much you would enjoy sharing your undergraduate years with these five friends. These are only a few of the academic and extra-curricular experiences that could shape your life into the future.

Now, given the wild end to my undergraduate years, I want you to expect the worst. By the rare chance that a deadly respiratory disease rapidly spreads across the entire world in the final months of your senior year, you will want to be prepared. First, pay attention in your biology classes (knowing your love for science, this shouldn't be a problem!), because you'll enjoy the experience of applying your epidemiology studies to this world health crisis. Second, if Notre Dame and the rest of the country shut down, causing you to finish your undergraduate years away from campus and apart from your classmates, be ready to embrace heartache and to anticipate different post-graduate plans. Finally, if you happen to be named valedictorian during that historic moment in Notre Dame history, be ready to offer your life as a model of hope in a very troubled time.

This crisis four years down the road shouldn't scare you or change your approach to student life at Our Lady's University. You have always been one to see every occasion—whether a celebration or a crisis—as an opportunity. So just be yourself, Brady Stiller, and you will be surprised at what results.

In Notre Dame,

Your Future Self

Brady Stiller '20

Originally from Madisonville, Louisiana, Brady Stiller graduated from Notre Dame as valedictorian of the class of 2020. Throughout his undergraduate years he studied Biological Sciences and Theology and was a resident of Dunne Hall. During his senior year, he wrote a 200-page thesis on the British author G. K. Chesterton, which he will have published as a book in 2023. After undergrad, Brady returned to Notre Dame for the Master of Nonprofit Administration program in the Mendoza College of Business.

It's not a race, It's a journey

Dear Freshman Self,

Can you believe it? It is almost time for you to take your first steps as an undergraduate at Notre Dame. From my time here in South Bend, I can truthfully say that college will be some of the best years of your life. You will meet people from all over the world, learn so many new things, and most excitingly, find your niche, your community at Notre Dame.

However, all of these great experiences and memories do not happen instantly. These sorts of things take time, a lot of time. Coming out of high school, you were at the top of your class, had lots of friends, and were simply comfortable with how life was. Now, coming to an entirely new campus and having to start over again can be a very frightening experience. I know that you will have doubts about finding your own way and striving to succeed at the same time.

Remember, though, that it's not a race. It's a journey.

Countless obstacles and barriers will seem to constantly prevent you from achieving your goals. Stick with them. It is easy to fall into the trap of comparing yourself to your peers. Trust me when I say you will feel like you are the only person that is not getting good grades, that is not making friends, that is not having the perfect start to college, etc.

But people always put their best moments first, so when you are wondering why your freshman year does not seem as carefree and life-changing as the people around you, remember that everyone is going through their own struggles. Everyone's college experience looks different, and there is definitely no "right way" to do college.

You will be okay. You are stronger than you know and the struggles you are dealing with will eventually pass.

As long as you are yourself, the right friends will find you. Every moment can be taken away without warning, so dance the night away at that dorm SYR or go to a dinner at the dining hall with people instead of taking a nap. Life is too short, and one day you will wish you could return to college when times were easier.

Cherish these four years because they will disappear in the blink of an eye.

Wishing you the best,

Brandon

Brandon Chou '23

Brandon Chou was born and raised in Louisville, KY. He is currently studying Science-Business with a minor in Compassionate Care in Medicine in the Glynn Family Honors Program. A member of O'Neill Family Hall, he has a wide variety of commitments ranging from competing on the club tennis team to leading cultural student groups to volunteering through service organizations. After graduating from Notre Dame, he hopes to enter medical school and pursue a career as a doctor.

Ten reflections

Dear freshman self,

It has been a tough year for so many of us with the coronavirus and all that it has affected, including learning, social life, extracurriculars, family dynamics, and so much more. However, we can all look forward to a great year ahead. Here are my ten pieces of advice for a successful first year of college.

Never eat alone – Especially for those who live in student dormitories on residential campuses, it is important to establish a social basis for one's life. At Notre Dame, we spend four years living together communally. Whatever dormitory one lives in, there is a regular dining hall opportunity for meals. In fact, it is not unusual for residents of the dorm to establish a table or two that are regular hangout spots for fellow members of the dorm. The most exasperating experience for a new student is to go over to the dining hall and feel utterly alone because you cannot recognize any of the faces. That is why it is important to find the location of the favored tables for members of one's dorm so that one can simply sit down, begin a conversation, and presume that one will be welcome. It is even better to turn to one's roommate or next-door neighbors living in the dorm so that you can make the trek over to the dining hall together. It is not surprising that new students in college are sometimes anxious about not fitting in or having a difficult transition. The best advice of all is to quickly accept the advice that one should never eat dinner alone.

Find a quiet place—All of us need quiet privacy and a degree of independence. Many students going to college today have never had a roommate growing up. It can be an abrupt change to have to share space with one or more roommates. It is simply a reminder that all of us need a separate place where we can quietly mull over the day, think about tomorrow, and just relax comfortably in our own skin.

Don't be afraid to cry—For male students, it may be especially hard to express one's emotions around less familiar people. No one wants to seem like they are emotionally fragile or unable to cope with the reality of everyday life. But there are moments, especially in times of transition away from home, when it simply makes sense to cry and let one's emotions burst forth. It may be surprising to discover that other people can accept you on your own terms. Many people are especially touched when someone who is young and inexperienced feels confident enough to cry in their company. It may even remind them of comparable experiences in their own lives. The important thing is that one should feel free eventually to express the whole range of emotions, from hearty laughing, to stolid reaction to challenges, to weeping over some difficult information or unprecedented challenge. Crying can be good even if it is not how we normally want to be remembered.

Be proud of your family—It is always said that we do not fully appreciate how important our family has been in our early upbringing until we get away from home. The relationship between high school teenagers and their parents is sometimes fraught with difficulty. One should never allow concerns about status or reputation or other relatively unimportant matters to interfere with a straightforward presentation of his or her own parents as key actors in one's own life and those to whom one is ultimately responsible.

Learn all the names—Make the effort to learn all of the names of your peers. The more people we get to know and the more names we commit to memory, the more likely it is that we will have a rich and fulfilling college experience.

Don't settle for your present group of friends—It is important in college to reach out to people who would not necessarily be our friends and companions in our home setting. That means people of different ethnic and racial backgrounds, different religions or none, and people who have a different range of interests from our own.

Don't confuse your GPA with your self-worth—Whatever grades one receives after the first or second semester are only an indication of how one has done up to that point. They do not determine one's future.

Get active early—Some advisors in high school recommend that first-year students spend most of their time studying and avoid getting overly involved in extracurricular activities. It has been my own experience that one also benefits from finding a range of activities that one can enjoy and that can broaden one's social world. I suspect that all of us have a kind of limit on how much time we can devote to productive study. What we do with the rest of our time is completely up to us. I am a big believer in activities that put us in touch with people in our community, during break time or in the summer, people who live on the margins and who have life circumstances drastically different from our own. Higher education aims to develop the mind, heart, and spirit of the individuals entrusted to its care.

Listen to alumni stories patiently—Sometimes you will have visitors at unexpected hours who will want to share that they used to live in the room of the dorm where you presently reside. If you listen, you can have the sense that someday you will probably imitate their example and want to have open-minded, contemporary students listening to your war stories.

Study, worship, socialize, exercise, serve—Study is an integral part of an academic institution. Ideally, one becomes a lifelong learner. For those who come from religious backgrounds, the college years can be an opportunity for making fundamental decisions about one's own faith life. Socialization is an integral part of a healthy, satisfying, and happy life. College is great for late night conversations, the baring of one's soul to a trusted friend, and learning how to listen to the joys and struggles of others. Everyone knows that they should exercise regularly and sleep sufficiently. The important thing is to do it routinely and make it an integral part of one's life. Finally, service is one of the reasons we exist in the world – that we can enter into the lives of others, especially those less privileged than ourselves, and make a difference. The important thing is to get involved.

Monk Malloy '63 '67 '69

The Rev. Edward Aloysius Malloy, nicknamed "Monk Malloy" served as President of the University of Notre Dame from 1987 to 2005. Originally from Washington D. C., Monk Malloy is a triple Domer, having received a B.A. and M.A. in English and a M.A. in Theology. During his tenure, Notre Dame experienced rapid growth in the university's reputation, faculty, and resources. He also helped to establish Notre Dame –Australia and the Center for the Homeless in South Bend.

Be an activist for what you believe in

Freshman Tiffany,

I am coming to you, a near-sophomore, telling you that you're going to be fine. You're a fighter. Yes, Balfour and Welcome Weekend were two completely different experiences. Yes, you will find that you much prefer one over the other, I know you will think that someone pointing out your "nice Mexican hair" is the end of the world and reason enough to transfer. I know you will think that general chemistry will be the death of you. I know you will even think that leaving physics is the best idea, but you will find that your heart belongs there, even when you do eventually switch into computer science.

You will find the election season is hard. You wanted something so badly that you never got to see, and the effects are exactly what you predicted, if not worse. Some of your friends will be harassed for being Muslim, Hispanic, or undocumented. You're fine, though. You will find that this will bring out something that had been simmering within you for ages. You will realize that you are an activist, and that you believe strongly that every human being is valuable in their own right.

You will be homesick. Homesick enough to call your parents and ask for a semester off. You won't take that semester off, but you almost do.

But, soon enough, you will become adjusted.

You will find friends outside of the small circles you're afraid to leave. You will go on retreats that will make you cry because you love everyone you met so much, and they are suddenly showing gratitude for you. You will meet friends who you will spend late nights talking, laughing, and wandering campus with. You will make so many mistakes but bounce right back up, because that's what you do best. You will find a research position in physics. You will switch your major with all the heartbreak of knowing that both majors are right for you. You will take Chinese and love every minute of it despite the fact that you mess up more times than you can count in a five-minute span. You will find clubs with all of the people who made your Notre Dame experience turn into this wonderful thing.

In your freshman year, you will experience all the emotions that you need to in order to ensure you grow, not only as a person, but as one of the Fighting Irish. You will find your home under the dome—that I promise you.

Sincerely,

Your Future Self

Tiffany Rojas '20

Tiffany was an economics major from Duncanville, Texas in the class of 2020. She was involved in 1stG ND, Diversity and Inclusion on Student Government, the Fighting Irish Scholars, and a Multicultural Commissioner in Breen-Phillips Hall. She has participated in physics undergraduate research. She takes great interest in studying Chinese, hoping to pursue it as a minor or second major.

Just show up

Corey,

Welcome to South Bend. It's a lot different than south Texas, and that's okay. This adventure promises much, and I hope you eagerly embrace the good and bad. Looking back on my time at Notre Dame, three things continually emerge as blessings discovered too late. First, explore South Bend. Second, befriend your professors. Third, just show up.

My freshman year, I remember leaving South Bend to go to Chicago as often as I could. Not one of my classmates ever spoke about what South Bend had to offer. In fact, the city remained a mystery to me until I got involved with student government sophomore year. The more local coffee shops I frequented, the more charming the city became. The more events I attended in town, the more relationships I built. The more community members I spoke to, the more opportunities I saw for positive change through partnership. Bowling nights at Strikes and Spares bring back as many warm feelings as late night pizza at Reckers. Now when I think of home, I think of two places: San Antonio and South Bend. Invest where you are, and it will give back to you in multiples.

Professors always seemed so scary, like judges sternly delivering definitive assessments on my abilities. The thought of spending time with them outside class terrified me. Talk about being wrong! Some of my favorite memories are watching soccer games with athletic administrators, coffee with my psychology professor at LaFun, dinner in Jerusalem with study abroad faculty, or lunch with my friend's rector in town. Build relationships with faculty and staff. They're some of the most fascinating and kind individuals, and I'm thankful to call them my friends.

Lastly, just show up. You'd be surprised how many people don't show up—all for legitimate reasons too. If you show up, you're putting yourself in a position for success because you're giving yourself the opportunity to be successful. Don't be afraid what people might think, or if you feel you might make a fool of yourself. A lot of the time your presence speaks volumes to your interest and commitment in a subject matter, even if you can't speak eloquently on it. The best thing I ever did in school was show up to random events I never thought I'd attend. It's a great way to meet new people, develop new interests, and challenge your comfort zone.

Have fun and keep these tips in mind. Don't stress! Most things will work themselves out in time. You'll have a blast. The next few years won't be easy, but they'll be some of the most rewarding, exciting years of your life.

Corey

Corey Robinson '17
Corey graduated from the University of Notre Dame in 2017, finishing with a varsity letter in football and a degree in the Program of Liberal Studies and Sustainability. After a string of concussions ended a three-year playing career at wide receiver, he stepped away from the game becoming both a student assistant coach and Student Body President in

his final year. Corey co-founded a national non-profit, One Shirt One Body, with friend and creative visionary Andrew Helmin. One Shirt One Body promotes the pursuit of higher education through the donation of issued gear by college athletes into their local communities. Other honors include Rhodes Scholar finalist (2016), Capital One First Team Academic All-America (2014), and Indiana Bicentennial Torch Relay Bearer Honoree (2016). Corey is now living in New York full time working in business development at Sotheby's, the world's leading auction house. In his free time, Corey enjoys writing screenplays and playing music with his band Rolfs Aquatic.

It will be fine

During your first year at Notre Dame, the football team will go 4-8. You will only witness two home game wins, and you're afraid to admit you hate watching football. You sit through the games because you are trying your best to fit in. You think what the guys from your engineering classes told you is true: "if you don't like football, then you chose the wrong school."

When another student sells t-shirts reading "it's fine i'm fine" (in Comic Sans) after ND faces an especially brutal loss to Michigan State, you immediately order one. It's fitting not just for football, but for how you feel about your first year at school. If you grit your teeth and keep telling yourself that everything is fine, it'll actually be fine.

Sr. Mary, the McGlinn Hall rector, warns you during Welcome Weekend that you will receive your first ever B's in your classes at ND. You think to yourself, I'm too smart for a B. When you receive your first ever C's, you worry that everyone else is smart enough to handle the courses except you. You'll be disappointed to find that the ND Running Club isn't a good substitute for your high school track career. There are no other girls in it, and all the other guys are too fast to run with. You'll struggle to connect with the women in your dorm and your classes. It will feel like everyone has friends except for you.

After this disheartening first year, you'll resolve to try

even harder next year in classes, dorm life, and clubs. If everything's not fine, you can just force it to be fine. You'll think that a great ND experience is something you can earn through effort alone.

You take on the position of Running Club President and recruit new members to run with. You admit you don't like football games! You join the McGlinn Hall Welcome Weekend committee not only to welcome the first years into the dorm, but to convince yourself that you are welcome there too. You learn how to ask for help in your classes. You begin to earn A's through hours working problem sets with your friends, pulling late nights in the Knott Hall study rooms. But all of this is exhausting. You constantly worry that you aren't doing enough, that you need to study more, run more, and socialize more to be happy.

By senior spring, you'll feel like you have finally made it. You have a ton of friends in Running Club, you're part of the best group of RAs in McGlinn, you've accepted an engineering job offer, and you finally have enough time to sleep 8 hours every night!

Then the COVID-19 pandemic hits and this all falls apart. Your ability to force everything to be fine shatters. You move out of your dorm without getting to say goodbye to any of your friends or professors. Suddenly you have no control over your life or what the next year will bring. You're scared, exhausted, and lonely all over again.

It took all of this for you to realize you didn't have to carry these feelings alone. It took a global pandemic for you to finally seek mental health counseling. You finally admit that everything is not fine, and it actually hasn't been fine for the past 4 years. You unabashedly put a name on the fear and stress that has grown throughout college and final-ly peaked. It's anxiety, it's manageable, and you needed a bit of help.

One year after you were supposed to celebrate your graduation at ND with family and friends, you still haven't gotten to do that. But you have been able to apply all you learned at ND to the next phase of your life. You're awesome at your first job. You're a well-loved member of the Stamford Running Club. You talk to your best friends from McGlinn every Sunday on Zoom. You chose the right school. You even watch football occasionally. You manage your anxiety with gentleness and care. You don't have to force everything to be fine. You can just trust that it eventually will be.

Yours,

Olivia

Olivia Jaenicke '20
Olivia is originally from Staten Island, NY and is now an Optical Production Engineer at ASML living in Stamford, CT. She lived in McGlinn Hall all four years at Notre Dame. She loves hot yoga, trail running, and a good book. She plans to run her first marathon in Chicago in October 2021. She is passionate about engineering education for high schoolers, especially young women and minority students.

Listen, live, laugh, love

Dear Maya,

After a year at Notre Dame, here are the top three insights I've gained. Hopefully hearing them sooner will save some distress, but you've grown in the process of learning them.

You are not right. They are not wrong. As you've learned before in yoga, recognize the teacher and the student in every single person. You need to work together to learn from every person you meet to help develop your own perspectives!

Leave every situation brighter and more lively than you found it. At every moment of every day, you are exactly where you need to be, so make the most out of it! Don't spend time worrying about where you could be instead, but accept the present situation and give it all your love.

Don't limit yourself at college because of people back home! You are allowed to make new friends. Meeting new people here does not mean you are letting go of people from back home. Your friendships are limitless.

Additionally, never forget that everything will always be okay and there will always be people who love and support you. Always take on difficult things and always smile while you do them. You'll look wicked and inspire others to do the same.

Love,

Maya <3

Maya Ramp '20

Maya Ramp is a resident of Welsh Family Hall studying economics with hopes to one day ensure economic policy benefits everyone! Here in South Bend, she works at the Boys and Girls Club and loves to go to the YMCA and Bend Yoga. She is a lover of pranks and candy as well as theoretical math and racial justice.

The version of myself I first fell in love with

2020, a year that impacted every individual to some extent, could universally be described as dismaying, but individual perspectives can make all the difference. Although your senior year and freshman year of college easily qualifies as the most mentally challenging year of your life, you chose to look at it as something you truly became all the better for. As you searched for inner peace, your optimism taught you to celebrate the strength found in grief, happiness in sorrow, and the absolute triumph that follows being brave enough to be vulnerable and go to war with yourself

As I reflect on my first year at Notre Dame, I realize I would not be the person I am today without overcoming the challenges I faced as well as the difficult decisions that many were forced to make this year. I believe in times of tragedy, when the true characteristics of people become apparent. As I forget the bad, the good shines through and reminds me how beautiful the world is and can be. Being at Notre Dame has shown me that beauty, ever-present in the days spent watching the sunset in my hammock by the lake and in the amazing people I have met here.

The version of myself which I have grown to love over the past year is the one who prioritizes mental health by ceasing the unnecessary depletion of energy through death, fear, and the constant trauma-provoked worry. The premise of death has followed you since the start of the year and continued to leave you in its wake even in your short time at Notre Dame, creating scars that cut deeper than the physical wounds. The beginning of quarantine in New York had its own devastating elements of death swirling around it as hospitals filled and bodies burned, but it never cut as deep as when COVID-19 came to your doorstep. A piece of yourself, the endless love of a father, was taken away from you. You searched relentlessly for ways to heal, and in that ongoing journey, you learned how to love harder and express more. Coming to Notre Dame allowed you to open up and seek community in times of strife, instead of dealing with it alone. The tragic death of your roommate, Valeria Espinel, devastated the community and caused the fresh wound in your life to deepen even more. The rough patches during those formative times allowed me to find peace and learn to see the light in the darkest of times. For that I say thank you and smile on.

Tahira-Jahnai Vera '24

Tahira-Jahnai Vera grew up in Brooklyn, NY. She is currently a Freshman in the College of Arts and Letters studying Neuroscience and Behavior with a minor in Studio art. After graduating from Notre Dame, Tahira aspires to become a psychiatrist.

Spoiler Alert: You're Alive!

Hey Kiddo,

Yeah you. Look, I know it's a scary time. You're just a shy scrawny gay Asian kid from LA probably thinking: what kind of hilarious idea was it to attend a predominantly white university in Wheredoesthecornstop, Indiana? I'll tell you this- from where I'm standing, it wasn't as bad you think.

Sure, there are going to be many times you'll feel like you don't belong. You'll feel like everyone wants you to fail. You'll spend many nights wondering if you should just hide in a cornfield and leave society. And when things seem to start to improve, you'll be sent right back to where you started because of a global pandemic. And yet, I say to you: you're still pretty genius.

Because even though it'll suck a lot, the good moments will make you forget everything else. You will meet some of the most creative, talented, open-minded people- the ones you were looking for in high school. You'll take classes that change your mind about everything you've ever known and truly develop a passion for learning. And even though it's the corniest thing ever (you're in Indiana, everything is corny), you will find a home under the dome.

I know you're sitting there in O'Hare reading this and shaking your head, thinking of all the schools in actual cities you want to transfer to by sophomore year. Think again, stupid. You think that home is a place. That grey brick is no place to call home. That wet, slushy jeans are no place to call home. That a town with a severe lack of sidewalks is no place to call home. But you should know by now that home is not a place, it's a feeling. You'll meet four of your closest friends on your second night playing Apples to Apples (you won't enjoy it, but hey, you'll get free ice cream). You'll get to meet your best friend randomly at lunch, and guess what: you're the one who started the conversation. One of your favorite subjects will be theology (what the heaven!)- shocker, I know, but that's only where the surprises begin.

I can't tell you much more, I'm afraid, because the time-traveling mailman keeps checking his watch and I don't want to create some kind of wormhole in space. Just get your little tush inside that Toyota rental and get over here. I can't guarantee it will be easy, but you've got grit, and there's so much waiting for you. All you gotta do is wake up on time and show up. You'd be surprised just how much that will do for you. Okay I have about six essays I have to get to and a bag of popcorn that's calling my name (I've gotta stop talking about corn), so just fax me when you get the chance.

A happy scrawny gay Asian kid at Notre Dame,

Tris (by the way, you go by Tris now)

Tristan Huo '23

Tristan Huo is a rising junior studying visual communication design and psychology. He is involved with the Asian American Association, PrismND, and STOA Magazine. Born and raised in Los Angeles, he loves music, art, friends, and things. You can typically find him painting, swimming, drawing, walking, hiking, dancing, bopping, jamming, twisting, turning, writhing, and being a good person.

Editoritorial Team

Jin Rui Cai ('24) is a Chemistry major originally from Tianjin, China, and grew up in the 626 area of Los Angeles. He currently resides in Keenan hall and is involved with the Glynn family honors program, Psi-Radio science podcast, handbell choir, chemistry club, and the badminton club. Jin would like to dedicate this book to all students and their instructors, who have found ways to continue learning and teaching despite the ever-mounting challenges in a pandemic.

Felicity Wong ('24) is an English major concentrating in creative writing and an art history and philosophy, politics, and economics (PPE) double minor. She lives in Lewis Hall but is originally from Princeton, New Jersey. At Notre Dame, she is involved with the Institute for Advanced Study, Student Government, Arcadian Dialogues, and Project Fresh. Although she realistically plans to pursue a career in law, public policy, or nonprofit work, she is a lifelong lover of stories and hopes to finish her own novel or screenplay one day. She is particularly passionate about education in the humanities and arts, amplifying the voices of people of color and other minorities in those disciplines. Felicity would like to dedicate this book to her best friends at Notre Dame who have taught her what it means to live well and love powerfully.

Ciara Fay ('24) is a Biochemistry major and Irish Studies minor pursuing a pre-med track. She is a loyal Bullfrog living in Badin Hall but grew up in Westchester, New York. At Notre Dame, she is involved in the Red Cross Club, Compassionate Care in Medicine Club, Irish Club, and Biochemistry Club. Ciara is passionate about the research she studied in a breast cancer lab during her first year on campus, and her plans for the future involve attending medical school and working as an emergency medicine physician. Ciara would like to dedicate this book to her three siblings, Declan, Ailish, and Keeva, whose guidance and sibling-rivalry have played a large role in driving her ambition, as well as to her wonderful parents who work tirelessly to help make her dreams a reality.

Garrett Pacholl ('24) is a History major with a concentration in religious and cultural history and a special emphasis on the Middle Ages. He is a proud resident of Siegfried Hall but is originally from Atlanta, Georgia. At Notre Dame, he is involved with the Glynn Family Honors Program, the Learning Resource Center, and the Philosophy Club, and he hopes to work with the History Club next fall when it resumes operations. Garrett plans to pursue a Ph.D in History and one day work as a professor, thanks in no small part to the fantastic professors he has met at Notre Dame. Garrett would like to dedicate this book to his parents, his brother Jason, and to the wonderful friends he met at Notre Dame who have supported him and made him the person he is today.

Santosh Ponna ('24) is a Chemistry-Business major pursuing a pre-med track. He proudly resides in Morrissey Manor but is originally from Evansville, a city in Southern Indiana. At Notre Dame, he is involved in Club Tennis, the Glynn Family Honors Program, the Preprofessional Society, and the Chemistry Club. Santosh is passionate about the intersection of clinic medicine and healthcare policy reform, and he hopes to work as a physician in the future. Santosh would like to dedicate this book to his parents, his sister Rupa, and to his friends at Notre Dame, whose unwavering support has allowed him to chase his dreams.